Essential
Mac OS
El Capitan Edition

Kevin Wilson

D0936746

Elluminet Press

www.elluminetpress.com

Essential Mac OS: El Capitan Ed

Publisher: Elluminet Press
Director: Kevin Wilson
Lead Editor: Steven Ashmore
Technical Reviewer: Mike Taylor, Robert Ashcroft
Copy Editors: Joanne Taylor, James Marsh
Proof Reader: Robert Price
Indexer: James Marsh
Cover Designer: Kevin Wilson

eBook versions and licenses are also available for most titles. Any source code or other supplementary materials referenced by the author in this text is available to readers at

www.elluminetpress.com/resources

For detailed information about how to locate your book's source code, go to

www.elluminetpress.com/resources

Table of Contents

About the Author

Kevin Wilson, a practicing computer engineer and tutor, has had a passion for gadgets, cameras, computers and technology for many years.

After graduating with masters in computer science, software engineering & multimedia systems, he has worked in the computer industry supporting and working with many different types of computer systems, worked in education running specialist lessons on film making and visual effects for young people. He has also worked as an IT Tutor, has taught in colleges in South Africa and as a tutor for adult education in England.

His books were written in the hope that it will help people to use their computer with greater understanding, productivity and efficiency. To help students and people in countries like South Africa who have never used a computer before. It is his hope that they will get the same benefits from computer technology as we do.

Acknowledgements

Thanks to all the staff at Luminescent Media & Elluminet Press for their passion, dedication and hard work in the preparation and production of this book.

To all my friends and family for their continued support and encouragement in all my writing projects.

To all my colleagues, students and testers who took the time to test procedures and offer feedback on the book

Finally thanks to you the reader for choosing this book. I hope it helps you to use your computer with greater ease.

Chapter 1

Setting up Your Mac

Setting up El-Capitan is pretty straight forward. If you haven't already got it installed you can find a tutorial in Appendix A of this guide.

Once it is installed and ready to go, you will need to connect your WiFi or internet connection.

Create an AppleID if you haven't already got one. If you do and you weren't prompted during installation you can enter your Apple ID in system preferences under iCloud.

Also it's a good idea to set up Time Machine using an external hard drive to do periodic automatic backups of your data.

Power Up

The power button on the mac is on the top right of the keyboard on a MacBook laptop. On the iMac and Mac Mini they are situated on the back panel usually on the right hand side.

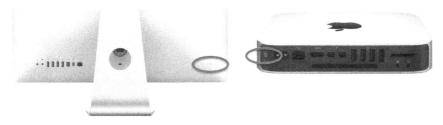

Press the button once to start up your mac.

Power Down

To power down your mac or send it into sleep/standby mode, go to the apple menu on the top left of the screen and select 'Shut Down...'

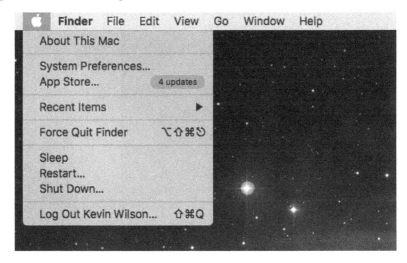

Your mac will shut itself down and power off.

You can also click 'sleep', this will put your mac into standby mode and is convenient if you use your mac on the go a lot and don't have time to wait for your machine to start up.

Starting your Mac for the First Time

Select your language. Click, the 'next' arrow.

Select your country of residence. Click continue

In the next screen, select your keyboard layout; US for the United States, UK for United Kingdom and so on. Click continue.

Select your WiFi network. Enter your WiFi password in the box that appears underneath. Click continue.

In the next window, click 'not now'. This feature is for transferring your files from an old computer. If you have old files to transfer, you can run the migration assistant from your Mac once it has been set up.

Click continue.

Choose location services. This service determines the physical location of your Mac so Mac OS can provide you with local information such as news events or weather. If you would like this feature, click 'enable location services on this mac'. Click continue.

Log in with your Apple ID. This allows you to make use of apple email, iCloud, buy music, films and TV programmes, a well as Apps from the App Store. If you don't have one click 'create a free apple id' and follow the instructions to enter your details. Otherwise enter your Apple ID email address and password then click continue.

Agree to the terms and conditions. Click 'use my iCloud account to log in'. This log you into your Mac with your Apple ID. Click continue.

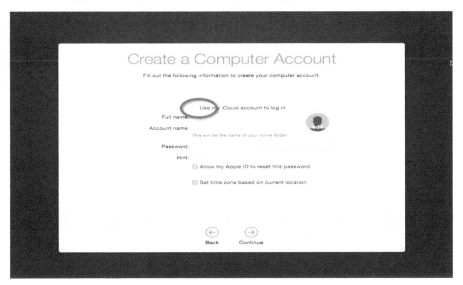

Click 'set up later' for keychain. Click continue.

Select your time zone. You can either click your country on the map, or select from the list. Click continue.

On the next screen, uncheck the selections for 'send diagnostic and usage data to Apple' and 'share crash data with developers'. Click 'continue' to begin.

Setting up Internet & WiFi

To set up your WiFi, select the WiFi symbol on the status menu on the right hand side of the screen

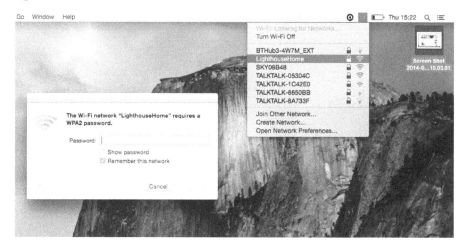

In the drop down menu that appears, select your WiFi network. This is usually printed on the back of your modem, access point or router and is sometimes called SSID

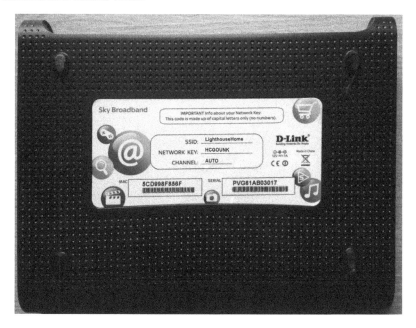

In the dialog box that appears on your screen, enter the WiFi password. This is usually the network key.

You can use the same procedure, if you are in a public hotspot eg library, coffee shop, airport and so on

If WiFi isn't available, and you use a cable modem to get online in your home, you can use a cable.

Here is a typical setup.

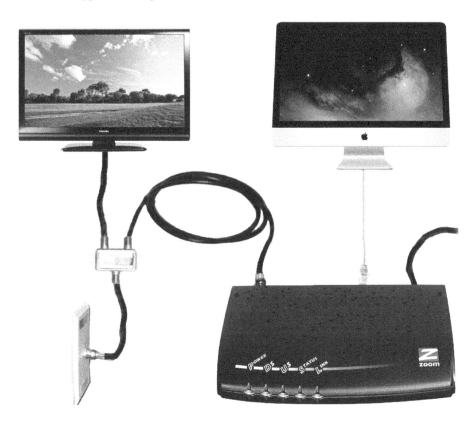

Your coax cable coming into your home is usually split using a splitter. One will go to your TV and the other will go to your modem.

Your computer will connect to your modem using an Ethernet cable.

Plug one end of the Ethernet cable into your modem, the power up your modem and allow it to connect to your ISP.

Plug the other end into the Ethernet port on your computer, as shown below

Go to system preferences and select network. Click on Ethernet on the left hand side, and make sure IPv4 is set to DHCP and your computer has picked up an IP address.

Connecting Peripherals

Most peripherals are connected using USB

On the side panel of the MacBook, you'll find your USB ports.

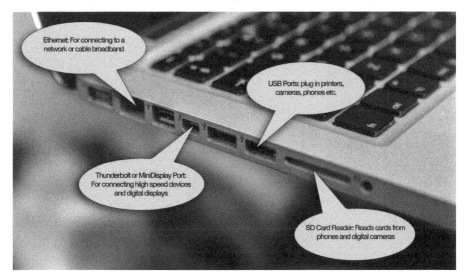

On the back panel of the iMac is where your USB ports will be.

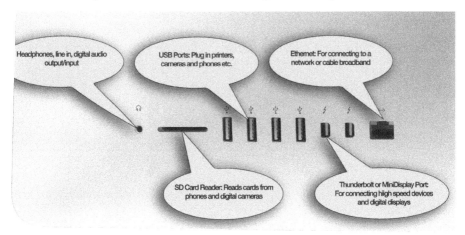

Add a Printer

Click on the Apple menu on the top left of your screen. From the menu, select 'System Preferences'. Double click 'Printers & Scanners'.

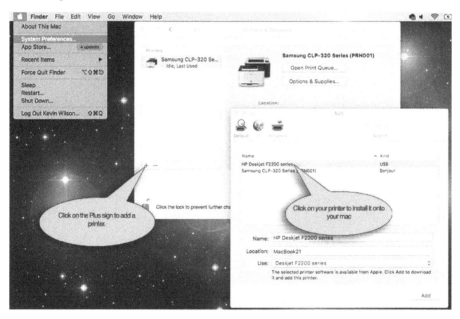

Click on the plus sign shown above to add a printer.

In the box that appears, El Capitan will scan for connected printers; whether they are connected via USB or WiFi.

Select your printer from the list and click 'add'.

You may be prompted for the driver disc that came with your printer, otherwise your mac will download the driver from its own driver library.

Apple Keys

Macs have a few special keys that allow you to carry out certain operations on your mac.

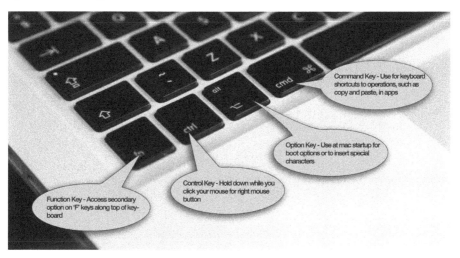

The Command Key

This is equivalent to the control key on a PC and allows you to use keyboard shortcuts for various commands available on the menu in different applications. For example, to undo something press Command-Z, to save press Command-S to print press Command-P and so on.

The Option Key

Also known as the Alt Key allows you to select which drive to boot from when your Mac starts. Useful if you need to boot your mac from a start-up disk.

The Control Key

This key allows you to use the right click option on your mouse.

The Function Key

This key is used to perform special functions with the 'F' keys along the top on a MacBook keyboard.

The Cloud

iCloud is an online data storage service provided by Apple. The service allows users to store data such as music and iOS applications on remote servers for download to multiple devices, such as your iPod touch, iPhone, macbook laptop or iPad. iCloud synchronises email, contacts, calendars, bookmarks, notes, reminders (to-do lists), iWork documents, photos and other data so you can access them from anywhere.

Creating an Apple ID

To create an Apple ID open safari and go to the website:

```
appleid.apple.com
```

From there click create an Apple ID and fill in the forms, then click 'Create Apple ID'

You will need this Apple ID if you want to purchase Apps from the App Store, use iCloud, Apple Email or purchase songs from iTunes Store.

Time Machine

Time machine is the Mac's way of backing up your files. Connect your external hard disk to a USB port as shown below. If time machine doesn't load, go to finder/applications and double click 'time machine' icon.

Setting Up Backups

If you haven't specified a backup device yet for time machine to use, it asks if you would like to use the external disk for backups the first time you connect it.

Click 'use as Backup Disk' and you're done.

Make sure you select 'show time machine in menu bar'.

Then whenever you want to back up, just connect your external hard disk and the backup will start automatically.

Restoring Items

To restore something click the icon on your menu bar as shown below.

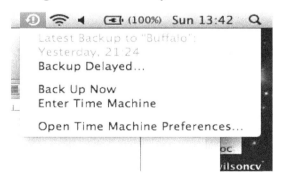

Plug in your external hard disk you used to back up.

Look for the file in the finder window shown; select what date to go back to on the left hand side

When you have found the file, click restore on the bottom right of the screen.

System Preferences

System preferences is the control panel of your mac. Here you can personalise your system and change settings.

You can find your system preferences by clicking on the apple menu on the top left of your screen and selecting system preferences.

Whenever you need to change a setting or a preference you should come to the system preferences panel.

Here is a brief explanation of what each of the sections in the system preferences panel does and where to go when you are looking for a setting.

Option	Description
General	Changes the general colour scheme of the OS (Aqua or Graphite), as well as placement of scroll arrows and font smoothing.
Desktop & Screensaver	Used to set the desktop picture as well as the screensaver, and their settings.
Dock	Adjust the dock size as well as magnification and position on screen.
Mission Control	Changes the preferences for the Mission Control application, such as showing the Dashboard as its own space or automatically rearranging spaces based on most recent use. Also sets Active Screen Corners and keyboard and mouse settings to activate certain applications such as Launchpad or to show the Desktop.
Language & Region	Set the default OS language as well as numerical, measurement, currency, date, and time formats.
Security & Privacy	Set "FileVault" and account security settings, and set up the firewall.
Spotlight	Set the preferences for the Spotlight system-wide search application
Notifications	Configures settings for notifications, such as the manner they're presented in (banner, alert, etc.) and which applications can display notifications and which ones can't.
CDs & DVDs	Used to set default settings upon inserting blank CD/DVDs, as well as music CDs, picture CDs and video DVDs.
Displays	Used to set screen resolution and colour settings.
Energy Saver	Optimize energy settings as well as set sleep times and processor usage. Eg set amount of time before screen goes off
Keyboard	Set keyboard settings, layouts and shortcuts
Mouse	Set mouse preferences. If using a Magic Mouse, provides preferences for the multitouch gestures like double-tapping with two fingers and swiping between pages.
Trackpad	Adjust tracking, clicking, and scrolling speed. Also allows users to adjust multi-touch gestures on newer MacBooks
Printers & Scanners	Set the default printer as well as scanner settings.
Sound	Set alert sound, volume and input/output options.
iCloud	Configure iCloud, enter apple id and password. Manage your iCloud settings and sync options
Internet Accounts	Add accounts from iCloud, Facebook, Twitter, Gmail, and other web mail
Extensions	Get extensions from 3rd party developers such as vimeo flickr linkedin and many more
Network	Set Ethernet and AirPort (WiFi) Settings.
Bluetooth	Pair Bluetooth devices and edit Bluetooth settings.
Sharing	Set the computer name for networked use, and setup file and printer sharing amongst computers/devices
Users & Groups	Control user creation/deletion, administrator privileges and user limitations.
Parental Controls	Manage parental controls for accounts, and view account usage data.
App Store	Previously Software Update. Set update options for your mac via the app store
Dictation & Speech	Set the computer's default voice, set up speech recognition, configure settings for the dictation feature, and other speech settings.
Date & Time	Used to set the date and time of the computer, as well as how the clock appears on the menu bar.
Startup Disk	Set the default disk, for the computer to boot into.
Time Machine	Set the Time Machine drive and backup options.
Accessibility	Make the system more accessible for those with sight, hearing and other impairments.

Adding Internet Accounts

You can add all your internet accounts such as facebook, twitter, iCloud and any email accounts you may have.

You can do this by tapping on 'Internet Accounts' in the system preferences app.

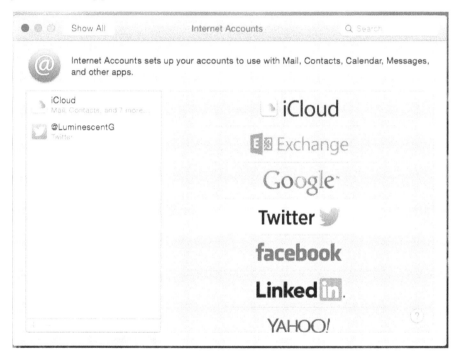

To add an account, tap the icon on the right had side. In my example, I am adding a twitter account, so tap twitter and enter login user-name and password.

When you add Facebook and Twitter accounts, each person's social media handle is added to a contact card in your address book.

Setting up Mice & Trackpads

Personally I find the default settings on the mouse and trackpad to be very unresponsive and hard to use. So I tweak the settings in the system preferences app.

You can get to the mouse/trackpad settings by tapping on the icons in the system preferences app.

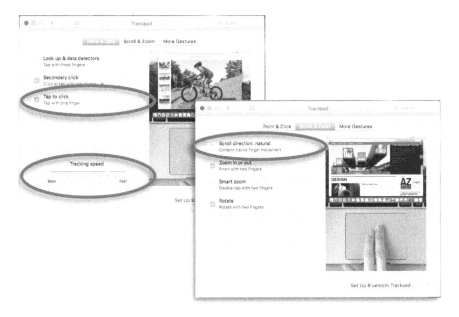

On the point and click tab, enable 'tap to click'. This allows you to use the tap feature to select something, rather than trying to click the left button on the trackpad. Also turn up the tracking speed if you find the mouse pointer really slow.

On the 'scroll & zoom' tap, uncheck 'scroll direction: natural'. So when you run your fingers down the trackpad your page scrolls down with you instead of up.

Chapter 2

Getting Around Your Mac

Mac OS X El-Capitan is version 10.11 and the twelfth major release of the OS X operating system for Macintosh computers.

El-Capitan's user interface isn't much different from its predecessor and still incorporates a flatter visual appearance with blurred translucent effects.

In this version, there are more under the hood improvements to the Operating System, with only a few visual tweaks to the interface.

Lets begin by taking a look at some of the features of El-Capitan.

The Desktop

The desktop is the basic working area on your Mac; it is the equivalent of your workbench or office desk.

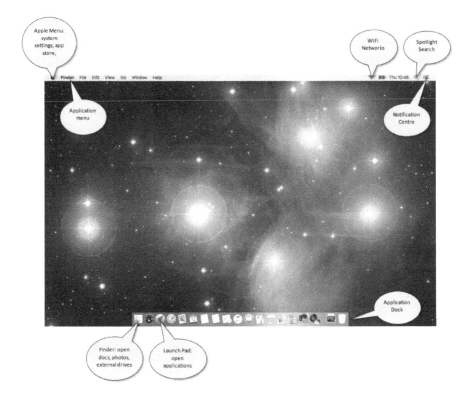

On the desktop you will find the Dock along the bottom of the screen, and a menu bar across the top.

When windows pile up, your desktop can get a little cluttered, Mac OS has a feature called Spaces, that allows you to organize your windows into groups.

When you're working in a space, your desktop contains only the windows for the work you're doing in that space. You can have a space that has your email and web browser open, another space can have pages or keynote open, another space could have iPhoto open and so on.

Press F3 on your keyboard to activate mission control.

Spaces & Mission Control

When windows pile up, your desktop can get a little cluttered. Mac OS has a feature called Spaces, that allows you to organize your windows into groups.

When you're working in a space, your desktop contains only the windows for the work you're doing in that space.

You can have a space that has your email and web browser open, another space can have pages or keynote open, another space could have Photos open and so on. So in effect, you have a different space or desk for each of your tasks.

Mission Control gives you quick access to your spaces.

To add a new space, click the plus sign in the top right corner. This will open a blank desktop where you can launch Applications as normal.

To get back to Mission Control, hit F3.

To shift between spaces swipe using 3 fingers on the trackpad on your MacBook. Or hold down control and press the right arrow key.

The Dock

The Dock has short cuts to applications, such as iTunes or iPhoto. If the app you are looking for isn't here, it will be in the finder or launch pad.

On the right hand side of the dock, are a couple of icons to take note of. These are what Mac OS calls stacks. Stacks are 'quick access lists' that allow you to find your most recently used documents and internet downloads. This is how they open up.

You can see a list of recently opened documents. Also is a list of downloads, so if you have just downloaded something from the internet you can find it in the 'downloads stack'.

If the documents stack isn't there, you can add it by dragging the folder from finder, shown below.

I find it useful to add my most used icons to the dock. You can do this by dragging them to the part of the dock you want them to appear. I'm going to drag my 'documents' folder from the finder window, and drop it next to the 'downloads' icon on the far right of the dock. This creates a stack.

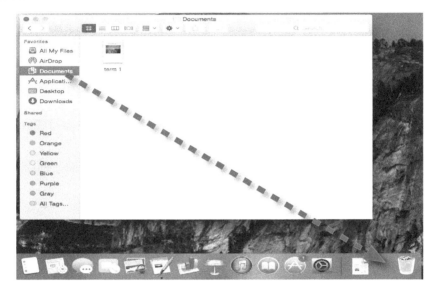

You can also add a program you use a lot to the dock. A common example is dashboard. You can drag the icon from the apps folder in finder.

I'm going to place it in between my Launchpad icon and my safari web browser icon. Just drag it to the dock.

Launch Pad

Launch pad lets you see, organize, and easily open apps installed on your machine. The icons are organized into pages.

To access launch pad, click the icon on your dock, circled above. To launch any application, just click on the corresponding icon.

You can organize your applications into folders in Launchpad. Just drag and drop one icon on top of another. For example, you can drag all your media apps together such as iPhoto, iTunes and iMovie into a folder.

This helps to keep applications of the same type together and makes it easier to find.

Then when you need to find them you just click on the folder when you open launchpad.

The Menu Bar

The menu bar can be found across the top of your screen.

One thing to notice about the menu bar is it changes according to which application you have showing on your screen. For example, the finder app will have its own menu, iMovie will have a different menu. Keep your eye on the top left hand side of the menu bar as it will have the name of the application currently running in bold type.

Application Menu

The left hand side of the menu bar contains the menu for the app you're currently using.

The name of the app appears in bold next to the Apple menu. There are several other app menus, often with standard names such as File, Edit, Format, Window, and Help.

Many of the commands in these menus are standard in all apps. For example, the Open command is usually in the File menu and the Copy command is usually in the Edit menu.

Status Menu

The right hand side of the menu bar contains the status menu.

This menu gives feedback on the status of your computer or give you quick access to certain features - for example; you can quickly turn on Wi-Fi, do a spotlight search, change your Mac's volume, see date & time, and check messages in notification centre.

If your menu bar is starting to get a bit crowded, you can remove items by holding down the Command key and dragging items out of the menu.

Finder

This is where all your documents, letters, photographs and favourite music are stored. The finder is like your filing cabinet.

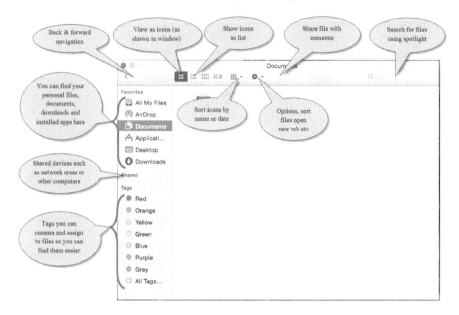

The Finder window is divided into three main parts:

The toolbar across the top of the window where you can customise they way files are displayed.

The sidebar which you can use to choose locations and devices on your computer.

The main contents, the large pane where all the files and folders are displayed for you to click.

You can launch finder by clicking on the icon on your dock

Tabs & Tags

Tags allow you to place descriptive tags onto your documents to allow you to find them easier.

Click your document you want to tag and select the tags icon, from the list select the tag that describes the category of your document, eg book samples, work, holiday etc.

To rename the tags to something more useful. In the Finder, click on the Finder menu, then click on Preferences

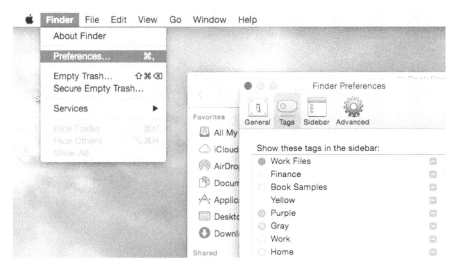

Click on the Tags tab at the top of the preferences window. You will see a list of the colour tags, and a few more at the bottom such as, 'Work', 'Home', and 'Important'.

To change the colour of a tag, click on the little bubble and choose a colour.

To change the name of the tag, click on the tag title, and type your new tag name.

Highlight a tag in the sidebar and you will see all the folders that fall under that tag.

Accessing External Drives

When you plug in a USB flash drive or an external Hard Disk, an icon will appear on your desktop.

Double click this icon to open the drive.

Note before unplugging the drive it is good practice to eject the drive clicking on the eject icon in finder.

iCloud Drive

iCloud Drive is Apple's file hosting service for devices running iOS 8/ iOS9, OS X El-Capitan, or Windows 7/8/10.

This feature allows users to save photos, videos, Keynote, Pages, Numbers files, and music online.

The idea being, you can start work on your mac and continue on your iPad/iPhone on the train, for example. Users get 5 GB of storage for free, but this space will be expandable via subscription.

Once you have signed into your iCloud account on El-Capitan, you will find a new option in your finder window called 'iCloud Drive'.

If you haven't signed in you can do so by going to system preferences, clicking iCloud and entering your iCloud username and password.

Follow the instructions on the dialog box and click next.

Here you can select what you want to sync between your mac and your iCloud drive. Eg, you can share photos in iPhoto, sync your contacts and email between devices, sync your calendar and notes all by ticking the boxes above.

To start using iCloud drive, you can save documents from any of the iWork Applications. For example, say you are working on a document in Pages, you can save it in the Pages section of iCloud drive as circled above.

Now if I want to carry on with my letter I can get my documents on my iPad/iPhone.

In your iCloud drive App, you will find the same folders as shown above.

The document was saved in the Pages folder. If you tap in the pages folder you will find your saved document.

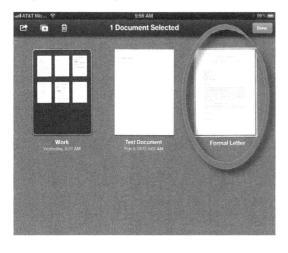

Dashboard

A useful utility that contains "widgets" which are small applications designed to accomplish a single task, such as a calculator, dictionary, clock, translator, calendar etc.

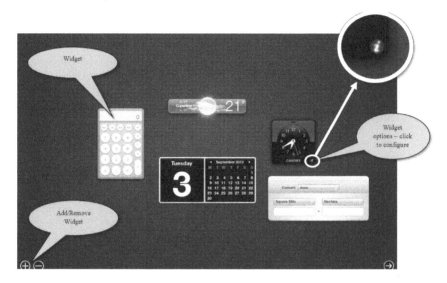

There are hundreds of widgets available; to add more click the plus sign on the bottom left hand side of dashboard's screen (shown above).

You can add more widgets to your dashboard by clicking 'more widgets'. Browse through the categories. Select a widget and click the download button.

Spotlight Search

Spotlight is a search engine that allows you to locate anything on your mac by typing it in. In El Capitan, spotlight has been extended to include results from web searches.

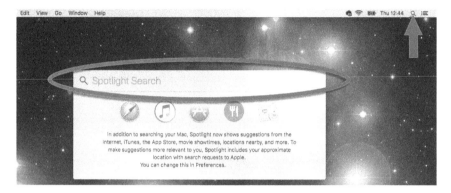

If you look in the top right hand corner of the screen, you'll see what looks like a magnifying glass. Click the icon and type in what you're searching for.

If you look down the left hand side of the window that appears, spotlight automatically sorts out the different types of files, such as documents, photographs, email messages and web searches into different sections to make it easier to find.

Spotlight can also give you definitions of words.

45

Notification Centre

Notification Centre provides an overview of alerts from applications and displays notifications until the user completes an associated action, rather than requiring instant resolution and can be found by clicking the icon in the top right of the screen.

Notification centre is split into two tabs.

The tab marked 'today' - shown below, gives you the current date, day, your calendar at a glance, any upcoming appointments and apps.

As you can see here there is a site meeting coming up as a reminder. The current time is highlighted in red.

Further down you can see upcoming events for tomorrow.

You can even add local weather by clicking on the green plus sign and adding your post/zip code if location services doesn't automatically find your location.

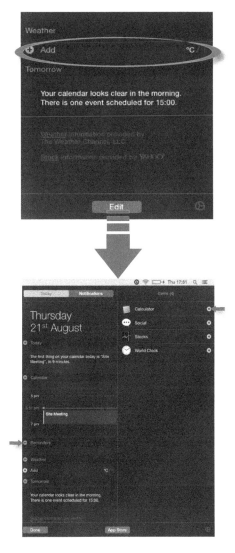

You can also add apps by clicking 'edit' at the bottom of the window. Just click the little green plus sign next to the app you want to add - shown above.

To remove any apps just click the red minus sign next to the App.

You can also download additional apps from the app store by clicking 'app store' at the bottom.

The second tab is your list of notifications such as new email, new tweets, new events, current iTunes tracks etc. There are three types of notifications: banners, alerts, and badges.

Banners

These are displayed for a short period in the upper right corner of the Mac's screen, and then slide off to the right.

The application's icon is displayed on the left side of the banner, while the message from the application will be displayed on the right side.

Alerts

Same as banners, except an alert has a call to action on the right hand side and will not disappear from the screen until the user takes action.

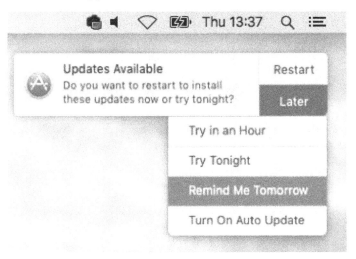

Badges

These are red notification icons that are displayed on the application's icon. They indicate the number of items available for the application.

You can change these settings by opening notification center and clicking on the settings icon on the bottom right of the window - shown below.

This allows you to set how the alerts and notifications appear on your screen when events happen.

For example email messages shown below appear in a banner on the top right hand side of the screen when a new message comes in.

It shows you the sender's name, subject and the first line of two of the message. To read the whole message click on the banner before it disappears.

Most of these settings you wont need to change.

Mail Drop

Mail Drop is a new feature in El-Capitan and makes sending large attachments easier.

Mail Drop will automatically upload large attachments to iCloud instead of your email provider ie Gmail, Yahoo, AOL or Exchange etc.

If your recipient also uses Mail in El-Capitan, they'll download the attachment normally, and if not, they'll get a download link that's accessible for 30 days. These attachments don't count towards your iCloud storage limits, which is great. Smaller attachments are sent as normal.

You can open and compose a new email as normal and attach a file. In this example the file is 80MB which is pretty large for an email attachment.

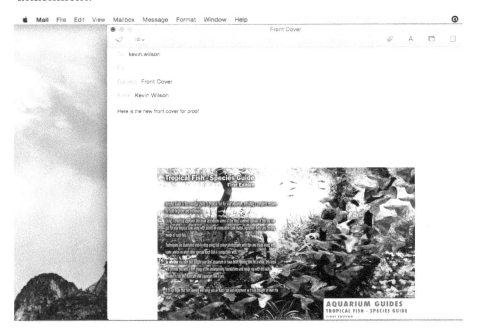

When your recipient receives the email, they'll get a link to click on to access and download the attachment.

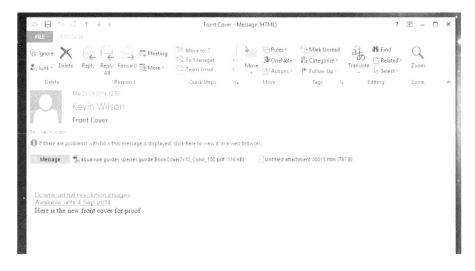

Air Drop

AirDrop is a service that enables users to transfer files to another supported devices ie Mac computer and iPad or iPhone without using email or a USB stick or external hard drive.

For example, in safari click the share icon and select AirDrop.

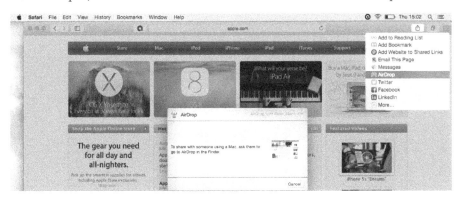

This will share the current web page with other AirDrop users close by. You can also share documents or photos in finder, by right clicking on the file, clicking share, then AirDrop.

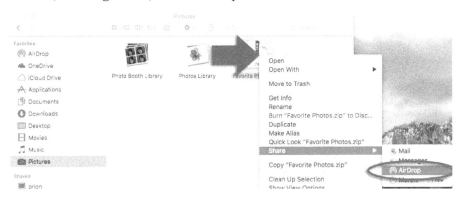

Your friend will see something like this

Handoff

Handoff is continuity feature whereby you can start writing an email on your Mac at your desk, and then you can get up and carry on working on the same email from your iPhone/iPad, without having to load it up or find it again to do so.

Handoff works between all your Mac OS X and iOS devices that are signed in with the same Apple ID.

You can enable Handoff on your phone by opening the Settings app from your home screen. Tap General, then 'Handoff & Suggested Apps', then tap Handoff to set it to On.

To enable on your Mac go to the System Preferences. Tap Bluetooth and turn it on, go back to System Preferences and tap General, Click the Check box next to "Allow Handoff between this Mac and your iCloud Devices"

If you open Mail app on your mac and start typing an email and then go over to your iPhone, you'll notice a small icon on the bottom left of the lock screen. Slide this icon upwards with your finger to go into the app, where you left off on the Mac.

If your iPhone is already unlocked, double tap your home button, swipe any open apps to the left until you see the handoff screen. Tap to go straight to the app.

Mac Phone

Now you can make and receive iPhone calls on your Mac. When your iPhone rings, you'll get a notification on your Mac showing you the caller's name, number and profile picture.

Click 'accept' on the notification to answer, and your Mac becomes a speaker phone.

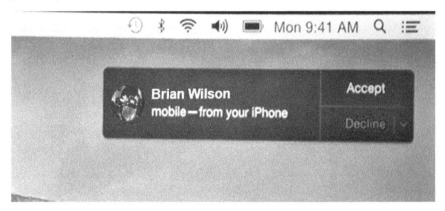

You can also use it with other smart phones such as android, but you need to download an app from the app store called Connect.

The Connect App lets you make and receive phone calls from your Mac, using a bluetooth hands-free connection to your phone. You can access Connect through the OS X menu bar.

Connect works with any modern smartphone.

Instant HotSpot

Instant Hotspot allows you to share your iPhone's internet connection easily with your Mac.

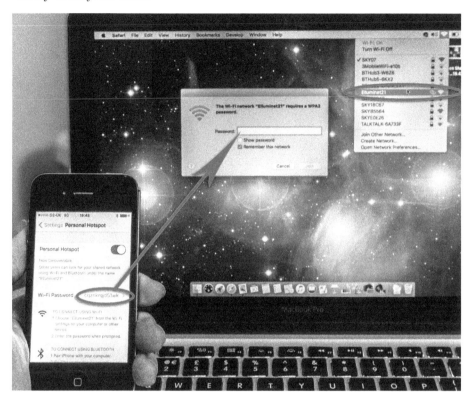

On your iPhone go to settings and tap 'personal hotspot'. Toggle 'personal hotspot' to on and enable your bluetooth.

Your phone appears in the WiFi menu on your Mac as another network. In this example the iPhone is called 'Elluminet21', so I'd select that one from the WiFi networks.

When prompted enter the WiFi password shown on your phone as illustrated above.

Accessing CDs/DVDs

More often than not, Mac OS will automatically detect a CD/DVD you have inserted and load up the appropriate App, eg DVD player for DVDs, iTunes for music CDs or it will ask you.

If not you can find the disk in finder.

There will also be an icon on the desktop representing the CD/DVD.

To eject the CD/DVD there is an eject button on the top right of the Mac keyboard.

External Drives

When you plug in a USB flash drive or an external Hard Disk, you can find it in finder listed under devices.

Open Finder to access the drive

There will also be an icon representing the drive on the desktop

Note before unplugging the drive it is good practice to eject the drive clicking on the eject icon in finder

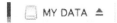

The Mac Keyboard

The Mac keyboard is not much different from a standard computer keyboard, although there are a few keys to take note of. These are highlighted below.

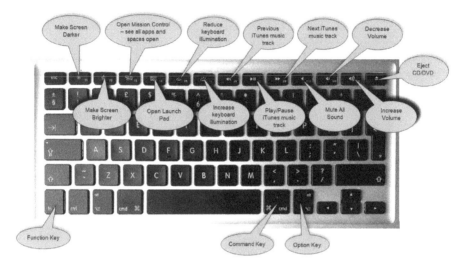

The fn (function key) is useful when you need to access a second option on the function keys along the top of the keyboard.

The cmd (command key) is useful for keyboard shortcuts eg copy and paste (Command C & Command V)

Making Gestures

If you have a Macbook with a trackpad, you can use a number of finger gestures to operate certain features of El Capitan.

One Finger Point and Tap

You can move your mouse pointer across the screen by using one finger on the trackpad. Tap your finger on the pad to select an icon and is the equivalent of your left mouse click.

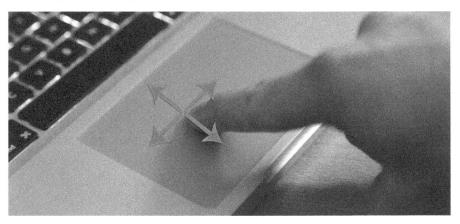

Two Finger Scroll

You can scroll down web pages and documents using two fingers on the track pad.

Two Finger Rotate

You can rotate things on the screen by using your forefinger and thumb on the trackpad making a twisting action with your wrist. This works well when viewing photographs or browsing a map.

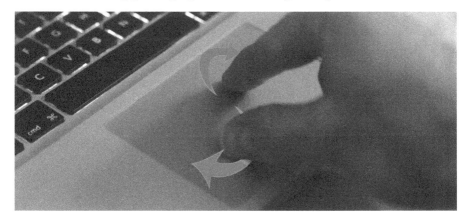

Two Finger Swipe

Swiping two fingers across the trackpad swipes between pages in a document, book or on a website.

Four Finger Open Launch Pad

Use your thumb and three fingers on the trackpad and draw your fingers and thumb together will open launch pad where you can select an app to open.

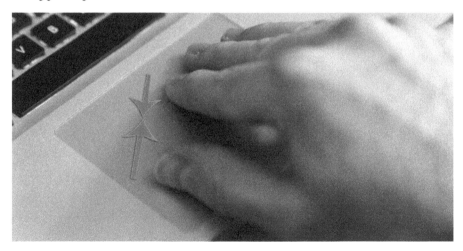

Magic Mouse

A Bluetooth wireless mouse with multi gesture support. We'll take a look at these gestures below.

Left Click

Primary select button to click or double click on an icon

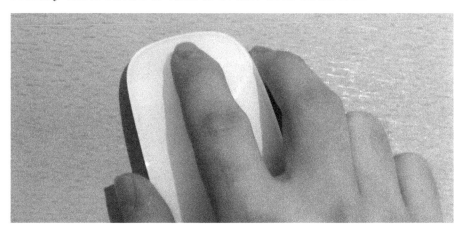

Right Click

Secondary click or right mouse button click to reveal context menus.

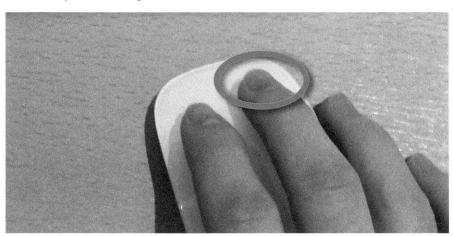

Scrolling

Scroll vertically or horizontally around a page, image, document, etc. Run your finger over the surface of the mouse; up and down, left and right to scroll pages

Swipe

Use two fingers to swipe left and right across the surface of the mouse to move a page forward or backward when reading a document or website.

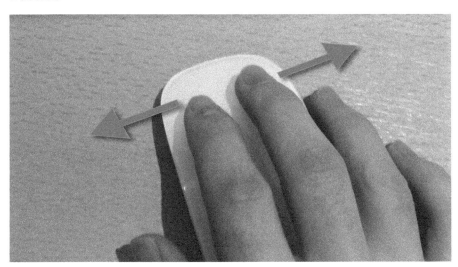

Using Applications

El Capitan comes with a good number of Applications pre-installed, from Maps to Photographs to Word Processors to Internet and email.

There are a wide variety of Applications or Apps available for the Mac that can be purchased and downloaded from the App Store.

Applications on El-Capitan can be found in a number of different places. Finder/Applications, the Dock or Launch Pad.

The easiest place to find them is on Launch Pad and the Dock.

Launching Your Applications

You can find applications on the dock at the bottom of your screen.

You can also find apps by hitting the Launch Pad icon on the dock.

If there are apps you use a lot, you can drag them from launch pad to the dock.

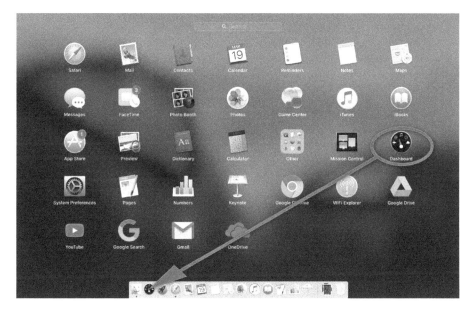

The next time you need the application just click on the icon on the dock.

Maps

Another great feature in El-Capitan is the maps app.

This allows you to find any location on the globe and is great for finding driving directions.

You can type the name of the city or venue you are looking for in the search field at the top of the screen. You can also enter postal/zip codes to find specific areas.

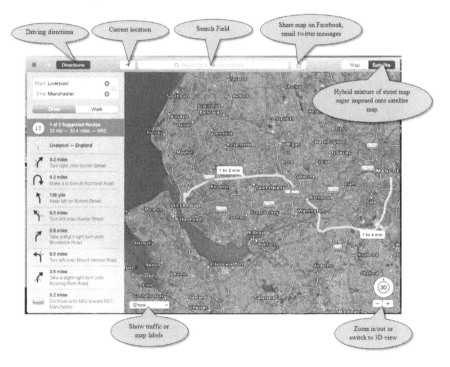

If you click the directions feature all you need to do is type in your location and your destination in to the fields shown and maps will come back with a route plus turn-by-turn directions for you to print or sent to your iPhone satnav.

You can type in city names, residential addresses and so on.

iBooks

To open iBooks on your mac, click the iBooks icon on your dock

Hit 'get started' and go to iBook Store. Once opened, you can search for a particular book by typing author or title into the search field on the top right of the screen. Alternatively, you can search through the categories on the top bar.

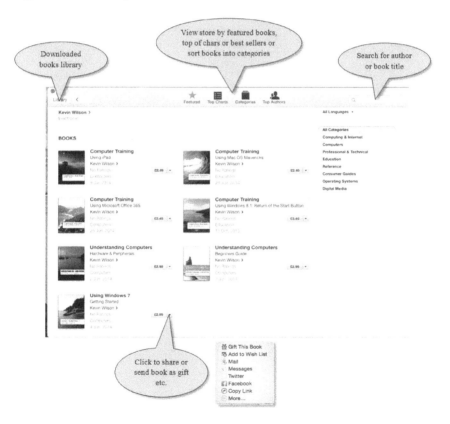

Once you have found a book you want, click the price, this will download it and add it to your bookshelf in your library. You can find all your books that you have purchased, by clicking the library button on the top left of the screen. All your books are synchronized across all your apple devices; iPhone, iPad and iBooks on your Mac.

App Store

The App Store is a convenient way to buy and install applications onto your Mac without the need for DVDs.

To access the App Store go up to your apple menu on the very top left of the screen and click App Store

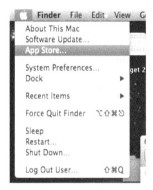

This will bring up the main store screen.

To buy anything just click the price then click install app and sign in with your App Store/iTunes account.

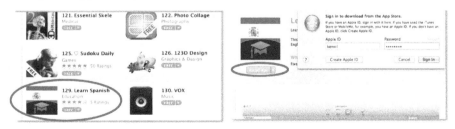

You can type in the name of the app you are looking for in the top right or browse categories

The app will download, and once it is complete, you can find your newly installed app in Launchpad on your dock.

Surfing Safari

Safari is El Capitan's default web browser. You can find the icon on your dock in finder applications, or on launch pad.

Launching Safari

You can start safari by clicking the safari icon on the dock as shown above.

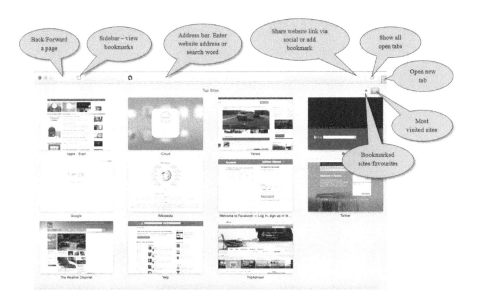

This will bring up safari's main screen, which will look similar to the one above.

Using Safari

If for example, I wanted to find Elluminet Press's website. Type it into the search bar. You can use a web address or type keywords.

You can use this technique for anything you want to find. Just start typing it into the address bar. It doesn't have to be a website address, it can be a keyword.

Bookmarking Pages

Bookmarking pages allows you to save websites without having to remember addresses or having to search for them again.

You can just click a button on the bookmarks side bar to revisit the page.

If you have found a website you like or visit often, click the share button

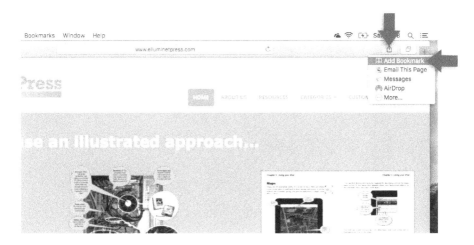

From the menu, select 'add bookmark'

Choose 'Favourites' from the drop down menu to add bookmark to your bookmark tool bar. I would only add your most visited sites to 'favorites', as there is limited space. Any other sites I'd add to the bookmarks sidebar list.

Choose 'bookmarks' from the drop down menu, to add the site to your bookmark sidebar list.

Using the Sidebar

You can access the sidebar by clicking the sidebar icon shown below

From here, you can access favourites/bookmarks and your reading list.

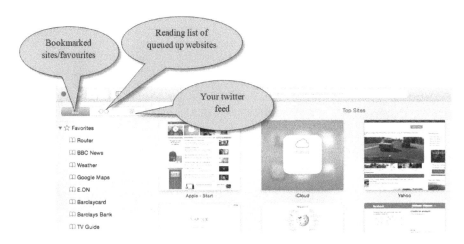

The reading list is where you can queue up a load of websites for reading later

Apple Mail

Mail also known as the Mail App or Apple Mail is an email program included with Mac OS. The main screen will look similar to this

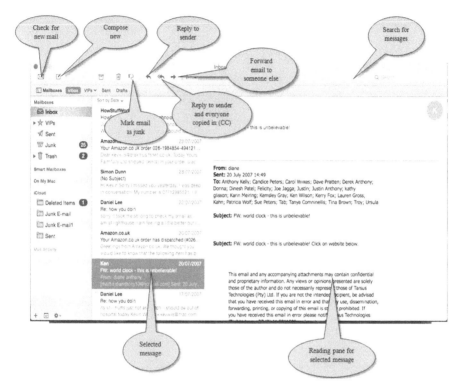

There are a few new features included in Mail for El-Capitan:

MailDrop and Markup.

MailDrop works by allowing you to send large files by automatically uploading the to your iCloud drive and sending a link to the recipient so they can access the file without clogging up the mail server with large files.

MailDrop uses your iCloud to store your files, and because iCloud is built into Mail this means that anyone running Mail on their own Mac will have the file downloaded automatically just as though it were an ordinary email.

Another feature added to El-Capitan is Markup. This provides a simple way of adding comments and annotations to file attachments in Mail.

If you send someone a photo for example, in an email you can activate markup mode, by clicking on a small pull-down menu that appears in the top-right corner of the image.

You can then annotate your image, type text, draw lines, circles and hand written notes on the image.

Below is an explanation of what all the different icons do.

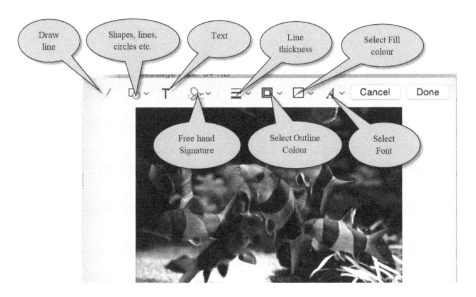

Once you have finished annotating your image click done.

If you don't see the pop-up menu, you may need to enable Markup. To do this go to your system preferences, click extensions, click actions, then select the Markup checkbox.

iCal Calendar

This utility is useful for storing all your friends email addresses, phone numbers, etc. These can be synced with your iPad, iPod touch or and iPhone. I find it easiest to view the calendar in month view as shown below.

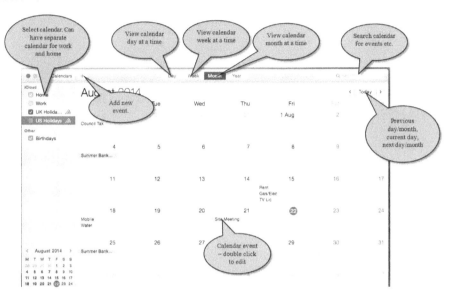

Adding an Event

The quickest way to add a new event is to click on the plus sign shown below, and enter the event name, time and day/date. iCal will then interpret this and add an appointment to your calendar.

As you can see iCal has interpreted the event and added an entry into your calendar. You can now add a location by typing it in

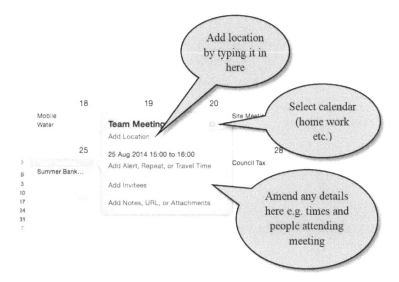

Add an Event from Email

Apple Mail scans your emails for possible events, meaning in some emails informing you of or inviting you to events, you'll see an option to add the event to your calendar. To add to your calendar, tap 'add' circled below/top-right.

A window will appear detailing the event.

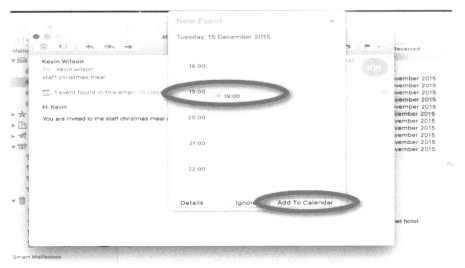

Click 'add to calendar' to add event.

Public Calendar

To add a public calendar go to the file menu and select 'new calendar subscription'

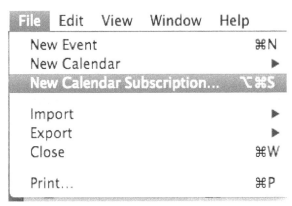

Then give it an appropriate name and enter the address as shown above. The addresses are below

```
webcal://ical.mac.com/ical/UK32Holidays.ics
```

```
webcal://ical.mac.com/ical/US32Holidays.ics
```

Contacts

This is your address book. You can create contacts, add email addresses and phone numbers. These contacts are synced with all your Apple devices; iPhone, iPad etc.

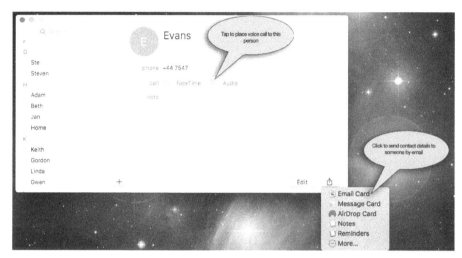

Add Email Contact from Apple Mail

The easiest way to add someone's email address is to click on the small down-arrow next to their name in the email header, as shown below.

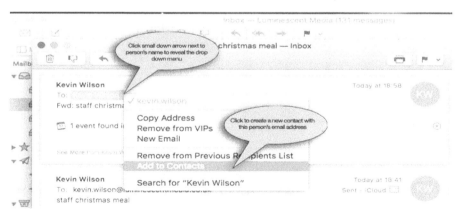

The tap 'add to contacts'.

Face Time

When you launch face time you will see a list down the left hand side of your known contacts. Log in with your apple id if prompted.

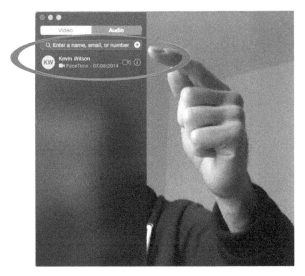

If your contacts are not shown here, you can search for them by either entering their name or phone number.

If they are available for FaceTime they will have a small camera symbol next to their name as shown above.

To make a FaceTime call just click or tap on their name.

You can see above a FaceTime conversation shown on both a MacBook and an iPhone.

If you are on a Mac, you can put FaceTime into full screen mode. To do this, go to the video menu and click 'enter full screen'.

Or press CTRL CMD F

Dark Mode

Dark mode allows you to change the look of the interface to tackle the problem of eye strain when using a computer in low light conditions or for long periods of time.

You can enable this by going to the general settings on the system preferences.

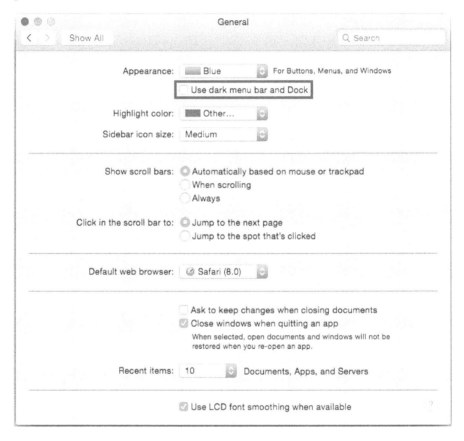

From the general preferences, select 'user dark menu bar and dock'

Dark Mode is designed to put less strain on the eyes and is intended to make reading a computer screen easier.

Here you can see the interface has a high contrast visual look with dark backgrounds and white text.

The dock along the bottom also shows up in dark grey showing up the icons a lot clearer.

Find your Mouse Pointer

If you have lost your mouse pointer somewhere on the screen you can wiggle your finger backwards and forwards across you track-pad or wiggle your mouse and your cursor will grow to a larger size making it easier to find.

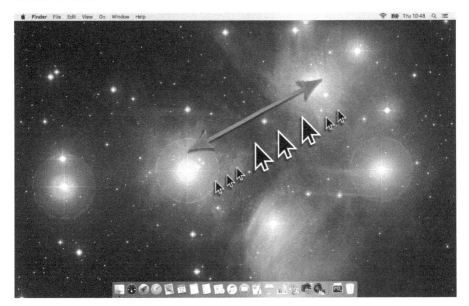

Image Capture

You can find the image capture App in finder/applications.

Down the left hand side of the window you will see a list of your installed devices; cameras and scanners.

Click on the device name to select it. On the right hand side you will see some information about the device. In this case the device connected is a scanner, so you will see an option to scan a document or image, preview it and save it to your pictures folder.

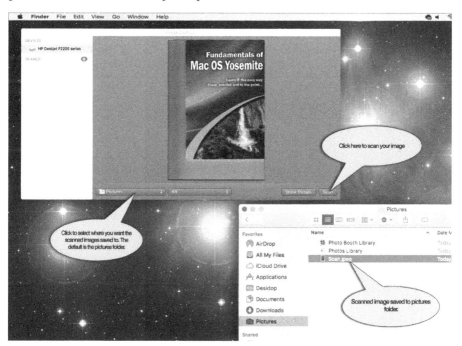

Photobooth

This is probably the most entertaining app that comes pre-installed on a mac. I had the kids entertained for hours.

Photobooth allows you to use your Mac's on-board camera to make face distorting images; pull a funny face or key out the background and find yourself underwater, on the moon, or a roller coaster.

You can take a photo using your iSight camera by clicking on the camera icon in the centre.

You can also record video, if you select the film strip icon on the left hand side.

The fun part is when you get to the effects.

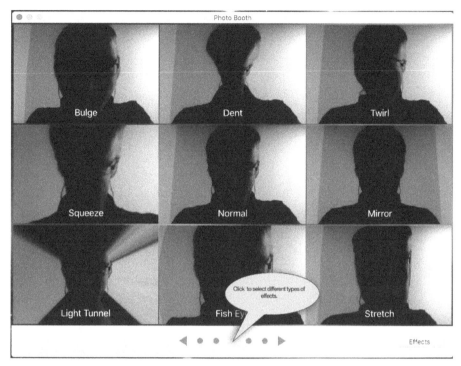

Select the effects by clicking on the image above in the 9x9 grid.

You can select different types of effects, from the distorted mirrors, shown above, to highlight effects or keyed backgrounds by clicking on the bullet points along the bottom of the window, highlighted above with the speech bubble.

Using Photos

Formally known as iPhoto, Apple have renamed the App Photos and have simplified the interface.

Photos has more features that are similar to the Photos app on the iPad and iPhone borrowing some of the same style of operation.

You can import photos from your iPhone and sync them with your Photos library as well as import them from a digital camera.

You can create some very nice looking photo books, greetings cards and slide shows all with your own photographs.

Getting Started

Photo is a great way to store and manipulate your photographs taken from a digital camera. First, enable the sidebar; makes navigating easier.

You can create albums and slide shows, you can email a photo to a friend, post them onto Facebook, you can even put together your own album send it to apple and they will print you out a copy and post it to you, these are great for family albums or wedding albums and other special occasions.

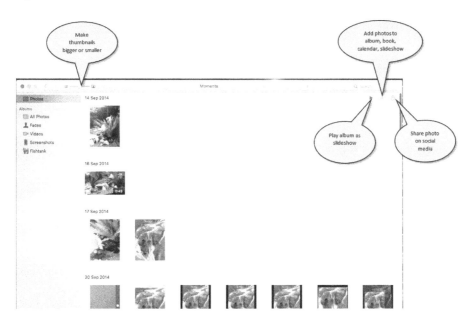

Photo allows you to organise and manage all your photographs, create calendars, upload photos to websites, create greetings cards, slide shows to music etc.

Importing your Photos

Most digital cameras connect to your computer using a USB cable.

Open photos from launch pad and connect your camera. Photos will detect the camera connected and open up the import screen.

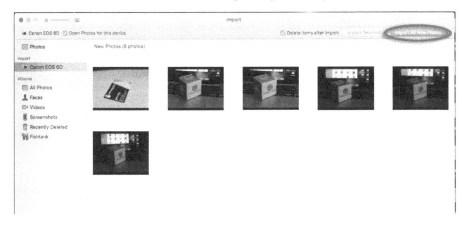

I found it best to delete them off the camera if I have imported them into my Photo library. This means I have a clean camera for the next time I want to take photographs. Do this by clicking 'delete items after import'.

This helps eliminate duplicate photographs in the library.

Now go to Photos in your library on the left hand side of the screen

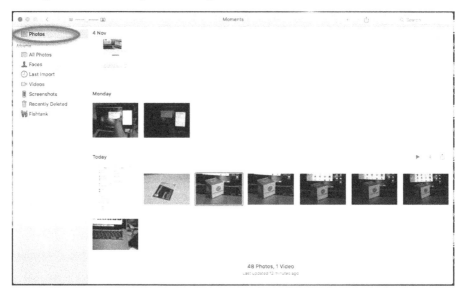

You should now be able to see all the photos you have just imported.

Now this is where you can put them into albums, create slide shows, upload to Facebook, email them to friends or create prints.

Manipulating & Enhancing Photos

A common problem I have come across, when taking photographs with a pocket digital camera, is sometimes photos can come out a bit dark.

To edit the photo, double click on it. Click 'edit' on the top right of the screen.

Down the right hand side of the screen, you'll see a list of operations you can perform on your photograph.

For example, to change the brightness of the image, select 'adjust' from the list of options down the right hand side of the screen.

Under the adjustments, you'll see one called 'light'. Underneath you'll see a gradient going from a dark image to a light image and a slider somewhere in the middle. Click and drag this slider toward the light, to lighten the image.

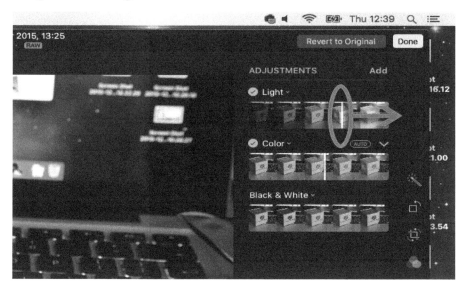

You can do the same for the 'color'; saturate and desaturate the colours.

You can also add extra adjustments by clicking on 'Add' on the top right of your screen. This will add another adjustment to the main list, you can manipulate it in the same way as before by dragging the slider. In this example I chose sharpen.

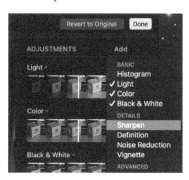

Try some of the other adjustments in the same way. To save the adjustments click 'done'.

Sharing Photos

You can share your photos from your Mac and post them to any social media platform you have signed up to.

From the main screen, select the images you want to post to your social media account.

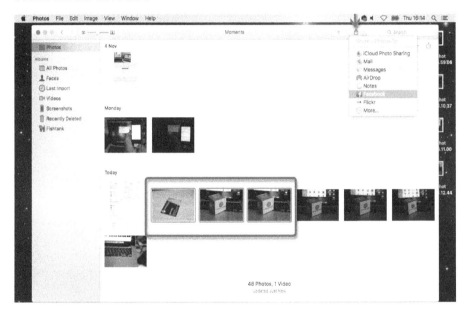

To select multiple images, as shown above, hold down the cmd key while you click the image.

Click the sharing icon on the top right of your screen, shown by the arrow in the screen above. Select your social media, in this example, Facebook.

If you haven't set up your accounts, Photos will prompt you for your login username and password. Enter these when prompted.

Click 'next', then click 'sign in'. Close the window and return to Photos.

From Photos, select the share icon and select Facebook.

Creating Photobooks

Select your photos from the main screen, hold down the CMD key to select multiple photographs.

To create a book, click the + sign on the top right of the screen. From the drop down menu select 'book'.

Choose the format you would like your album printed in.

There are a number to choose from as shown below.

In the next screen, you'll notice Photos has put all your images into the pages. You can leave the photos in this order or if you prefer, click 'clear placed photos' and all the photos will be removed and placed on the dock at the bottom of the window.

From here you can click and drag the photos onto the pages in the order and position you want them.

Double click on the thumbnails to enlarge them to edit text and adjust layouts.

You can adjust the layout if you want more photos on one page or a photo and a text field if you want to add some explanation/story to your book.

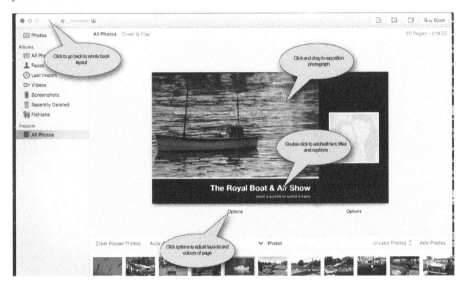

You can do this by clicking 'options' and selecting a template from the layout options.

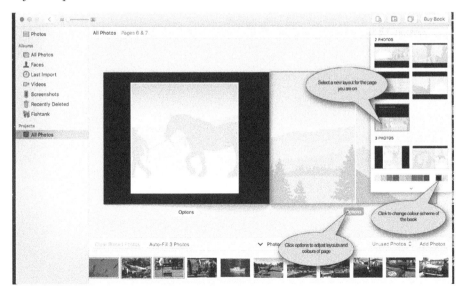

Once you are happy with the book, click 'buy book' to order your book as a hard copy printed album.

Click 'Add shipping address' type in or select your address and click 'place order'

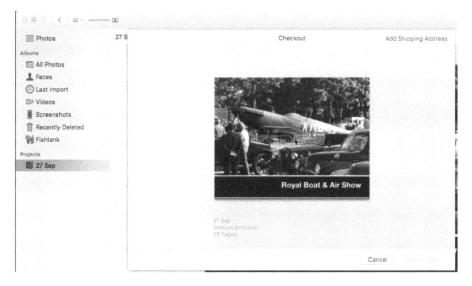

These make nice gifts at weddings, birthdays and special events.

Creating Slide Shows

Select the photos you want, hold down the CMD key to select multiple photographs. Click the + sign in the top right of the screen.

From the drop down menu select 'slideshow'

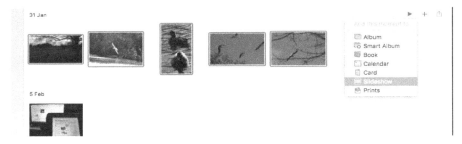

Give your slideshow a name

Double click the title text to edit the title.

Add some effects by clicking on the effects button on the right hand side, circled below far right.

In this example, I am going to apply a nice vintage photo look.

Click the music icon on the right hand side, indicated by the arrow, to add some music. You can add music from photos or you can use music from your iTunes library.

Hit the play button to run your slideshow.

Ordering Prints

Select the photographs you want to print, hold down the CMD key to select multiple photographs.

Click the + sign in the top right of the screen and select 'prints' from the drop down menu.

Ordering prints is like using a kiosk at a photo store where you can order professionally printed photographs. This feature of Photos works in a similar way.

Select from the list, the size of you photographs you want to print.

Select a glossy finish on the top right hand side of the screen.

All the photos you have selected will be scaled and cropped to the size of the photographs you have selected on the previous screen.

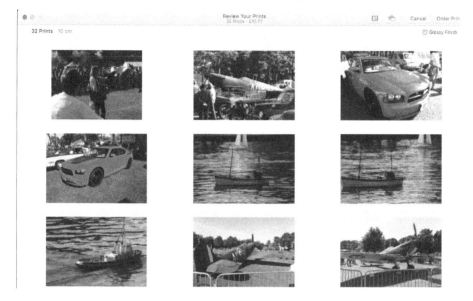

You can change sizes by right clicking on the image and selecting a different size from the 'change size' sub menu.

Once you are done, click 'order prints', enter your payment and address details. Then click 'place order'.

Greeting Cards

Select your photograph to make your card. In this example, I am going to use a nice coffee image.

Click the + sign on the top right and select 'card' from the drop down menu

Select the size and style of card you want. There are templates to choose from.

Choose a template, in this case I'm going to choose 'flurry'.

Change the text on the front

Click on 'inside' then click on the text box circled at the bottom and enter your message. You can also change fonts and colours using the 'text options' box on the right hand side of the window.

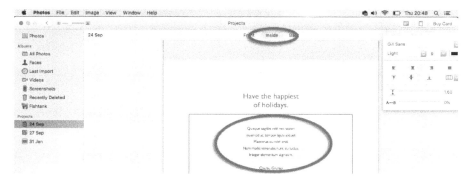

Once you are happy, click 'buy card' on the top right of the screen. Add your recipient's address and click 'place order'.

A Gift Calendar

You can make a calendar using your own photographs. Pick 12 photos of you and your family or of a special occasion and present it to someone as a special gift.

Select your photos from the main screen. Hold down the CMD key to select multiple photographs.

Click the + sign on the top right of the screen

Select a 12 month calendar - one photo on each page. Select 'calendar'

Then select the start month and year. Usually starts from January.

Hit continue

Select from the templates a style you like

You'll see Photos has inserted all your photographs.

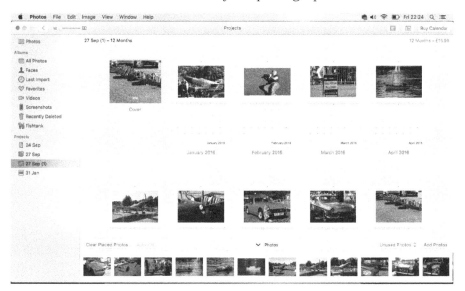

You can click on the thumbnails to change the layout. Click and drag photos from different pages to other pages to re-arrange them.

Click and drag photos from the strip of photos along the bottom onto the pages to replace photos.

Once you are happy click 'buy calendar'.

Chapter 5

Using iTunes

iTunes is a library that doesn't just offer music, but also movies, TV programmes and music videos.

You can use it to store all your music, transfer it onto your iPhone or iPad, burn it to a CD as well as go to the iTunes store and buy some of your favourite albums, tracks, music videos or catch up with the latest series on TV and stream it straight to your mac.

Lets take a look at iTunes main screen.

Getting Started

iTunes allows you to organize and manage all your music.

You can purchase individual tracks or albums from the music store or you can import music from an ordinary music CD.

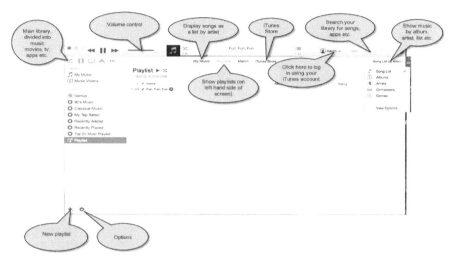

When using iTunes, I find it easier to use with the sidebar showing as above. To turn it click 'playlists' on the top centre of the screen.

When you plug in an iPhone or iPod/iPad another icon appears allowing you to view content and change sync settings for your phone.

Here you can check for updates, view music, add/remove apps, photos etc by clicking on the links down the left hand side of the screen.

Add Music to iPhone

To add music, plug in your iPhone

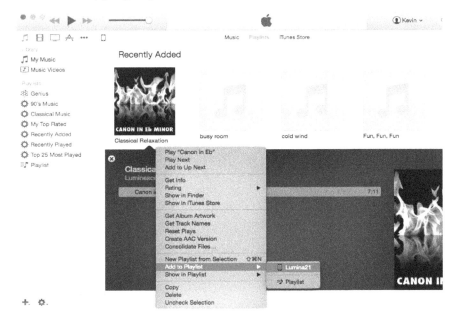

Find a track in your library, right click on that track and in the menu that appears, go down to 'Add to Playlist'.

You can select multiple tracks by holding down the CMD key while clicking the tracks. Then right click on one of the selected tracks.

Then in the slide out menu select the name of your iPhone.

Burn a Playlist to a CD

When adding music to your playlist, as a guide, keep an eye on the status bar at the bottom middle of the main window, an 80 minute CD will hold 1.2 hours.

Once you have compiled your playlist, right click on it in the pane on the left hand side. Click burn playlist to disc.

'Use Sound Check' is useful when you have a made a compilation of songs from different albums. It makes sure all the songs are at the same volume level so you don't have to raise or lower the volume too much when you're listening to the CD in the car or on a CD player.

Make sure 'Gap Between Songs' is set to none or automatic.

Insert a blank CD-R then click burn.

Import from a CD

CDs are a bit old school now days but many of us still have large collections of CDs with music we all enjoy listening to.

You can import music from a CD by inserting the disc into your drive

iTunes will scan the CD and ask you if you want to import the tracks.

99% of the time iTunes will be able to find the track names and album art for you.

Click 'yes' to import the tracks into your iTunes library.

iTunes Store

Click sign in.

Enter your iTunes store account. This is the same as your apple id or icloud id.

Click iTunes Store to start.

Once you are signed in type the songs you want in Search Store field on the right hand side of the screen.

Click on the price to download the song. Once the songs are downloaded you will find then in your recently added playlist.

Apple Music

Apple Music is a music streaming service and for a monthly subscription fee, you can listen to any music that is available in the iTunes Store.

£9.99 a month gets you full access to the iTunes store and many radio stations available. This is an individual account and allows only one account access to the iTunes Store.

£14.99 a month gets you full access to the iTunes store and radio stations and allows up to 6 people to sign in and listen to their music. This is ideal for families.

To get started, make sure you have updated to the latest iTunes on your Mac.

In the top-left corner, click the Music icon.

Click 'For You'. Then click 'Start 3-Month Free Trial' or 'Join Apple Music'.

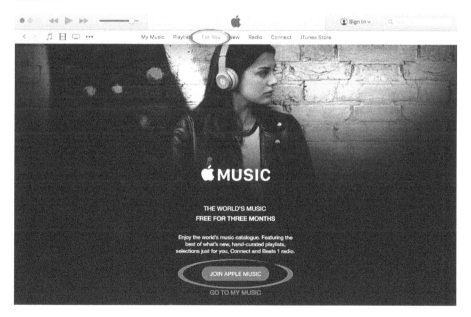

Choose a membership programme and sign in with your Apple ID

Select the genres you like. Click next. Select the artists you like. Click Done.

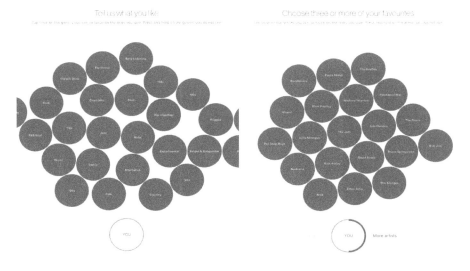

Select whether you want to upload your iTunes library. This is the library of music you have downloaded from iTunes and is stored on your Mac. Uploading this will allow you to access this library on all your devices (iPad, iPhone and so on).

Now, you can search for any artist, band or song you can think of. To do this, on iTunes's home screen, type an artist's/album name into the search field on the top right.

Click on the name in the search list. You will see a whole selection of albums, singles and songs you can listen to. Click on an album or song.

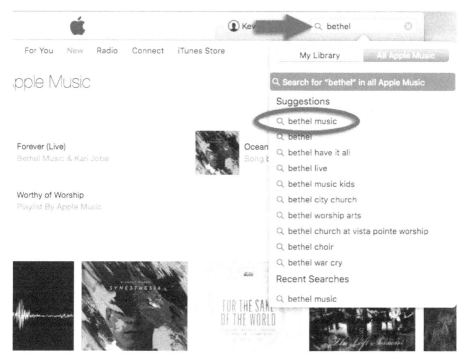

From here you can click on a song to listen to it, or you can build your own playlists.

Creating Playlists

To create a new playlist, click the + sign in the bottom left hand side of the screen. This will add a playlist to the library. Type in the name you want to call it.

Adding Songs

Right click your mouse on the song you want to add.

From the drop down menu that appears, select 'add to playlist'

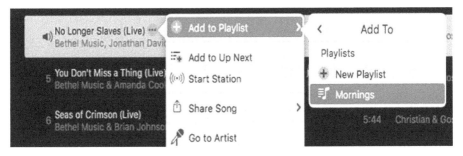

Then select your playlist you want to add your song to. If you have no playlists, tap 'new playlist' and give it a name.

Tap done.

120

Using Pages

iWork (Apple Productivity Apps), is an office suite of applications that include

Pages; a desktop publishing and word-processing package

Keynote for presentations

Numbers; a spreadsheet program.

If you don't have these applications on your Mac, you can download them from the App Store.

Lets take a look at creating a simple document using Pages.

Starting Pages

To launch Pages, click the icon on your Launchpad

Once Pages 6 has opened, you can open a saved document, or click 'new document' to open a new one

You will now need to select a template.

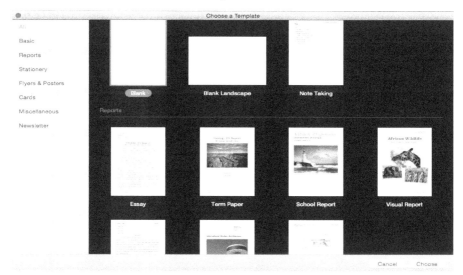

Once you have selected the template to use you will see the main work screen.

Let's take a closer look at the main editing screen.

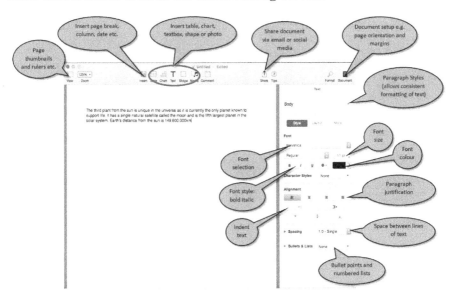

Formatting Text

To use Pages, begin typing in your text into the main window as shown above.

The text we entered before needs a heading. To add a heading type it in above the block of text.

Highlight your text with the mouse as shown above then click the small down arrow on the right hand side of the screen (circled above) and click title from the menu that appears.

Formatting your document means laying it out in a style that is easy to read and looks attractive. This could involve changing fonts, making text bigger for headings, changing colour of text, adding graphics and photographs, etc.

For each document template you choose from the Template Chooser there are a number of pre-set paragraph styles. These are to help you format your document consistently, eg so all headings are the same font, size and colour.

Adding a Picture

The easiest way to add a picture is to find it in your finder window

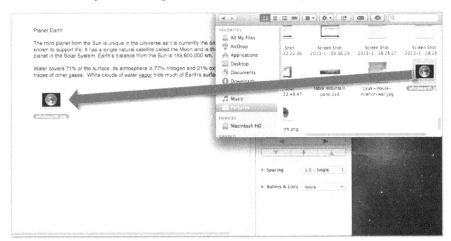

Then click and drag it into your document. It might be helpful to position your finder window next to your document window as shown in the figure above.

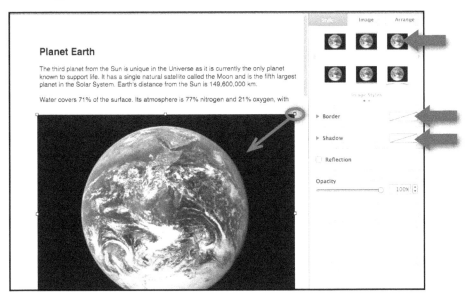

You can resize your image by clicking the resize handles, circled above, and dragging them. You can change the styles by adding borders and shadows by experimenting with the options in the style tab on the right hand side of the screen.

Instant Alpha

To get rid of these you use instant alpha from the format menu.

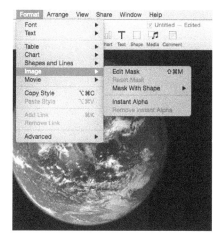 

Click in the black area around the image. This is the bit we want to get rid of.

To remove any similar colours that are not initially deleted. On the image click your mouse on the black area of the image and drag it slightly until all the black changes colour as shown below.

Saving

You can either save your work on your iCloud Drive or your local documents on your mac.

Go to the file menu and select save...

Down the left hand side of the screen you will see some destinations where you can save your file. Take note of Documents under favourites - this is on your mac. Also take note of iCloud at the top, this saves onto your iCloud Drive.

The advantage of saving to your iCloud Drive is you can access and edit the documents you have just been working on, on your iPhone or iPad. Or even another mac.

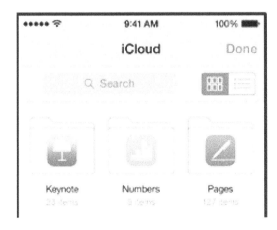

Chapter 7

Using Keynote

iWork (Apple Productivity Apps), is an office suite of applications that include

Pages; a desktop publishing and word-processing package

Keynote for presentations

Numbers; a spreadsheet program.

If you don't have these applications on your Mac, you can download them from the App Store.

Lets take a look at creating a simple presentation using keynote.

Starting Keynote

Keynote allows you to create multimedia presentations. To launch keynote, go to launch pad and click keynote.

Once keynote has loaded, you can select a saved file to open.

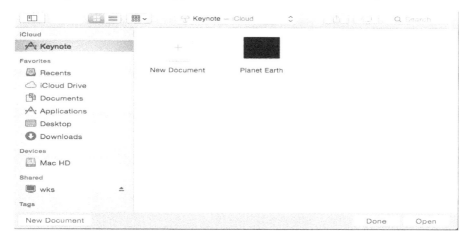

If you want to create a new presentation, click 'new document' on the bottom left hand side of the window. From here you can select from a variety of pre-designed templates with different themes, fonts and colours.

Once you have selected a template you will see the main screen as shown below. This is where you can start building your presentation.

131

Editing a Slide

Double click in the heading field shown above and enter a heading eg 'Planet Earth'. You can click and drag the heading wherever you like.

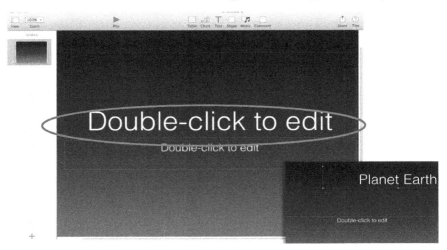

Adding a New Slide

Click the new slide button located on the bottom left of the screen

Click a slide layout from the options that appear.

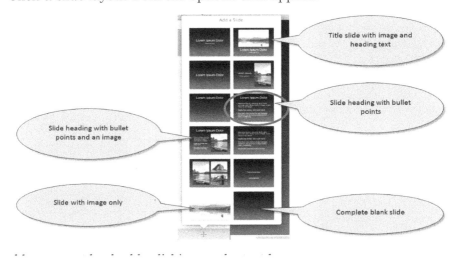

Add some text by double clicking on the text box that appears in the slide

132

Adding Media

The easiest way to add images and media to your slides is to find them in your finder window then drag and drop them onto the slides where the image is to appear

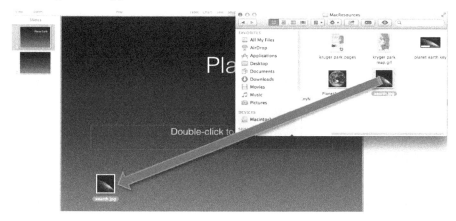

Browse through, to select the one you want, drag and drop the image to the slide.

If you want photographs, they can be dragged and dropped from your iPhoto library by starting up iPhoto finding the photograph in your library then dragging and dropping it onto your slide.

It helps to drag your iPhoto window over as shown above so you can see your slide underneath

133

Special Effects

In keynote you can add little animations and effects to your slides to make them more presentable.

Animations

Animations allow you to make objects such as text or photographs appear...

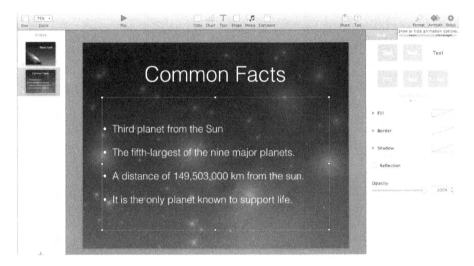

Click on your text box and select the animate icon located on the top right corner of your screen

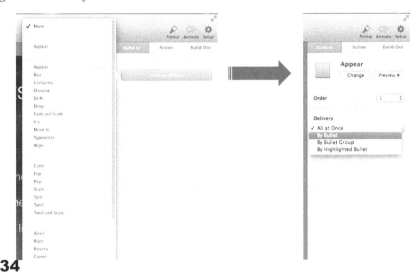

Then select an effect from the effects drop down menu (shown above left). Then specify that you want the bullet points to appear one by one. Click the box under 'delivery' and select 'by bullet' from the drop down menu.

To see what the effect looks like, click 'preview'

Formatting Text Boxes

Click text box to add shown below.

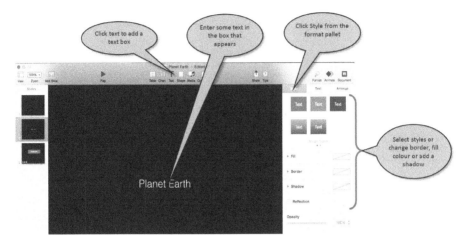

Enter some text into your textbox

You can format your text box by adding borders, changing fonts, changing the background colour, etc To format the border and fill click your text box and on the right hand side of the screen select style.

Formatting Text Inside Textboxes

To change the formatting of the text, for example to change the colour of the text or make it bold.

First select your text in the text box you want to change then click the text icon on the right hand side of your screen as shown below.

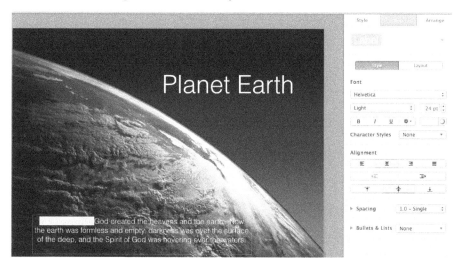

From here you can change the font, the font colour, size etc

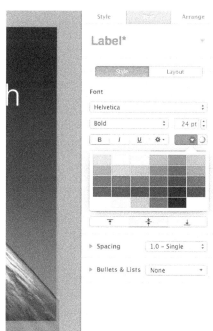

As an example I have changed the colour to dark red and made it bold

Adding Styles to Textboxes

If you wanted to change the background colour (also called fill colour) or add a nice border around the box you can do this by clicking on your text box then selecting style icon located on the top right of your screen

If you look down the right hand side you will see sections: 'Fill' allows you to change the background colour of the text box. 'Border' allows you to add fancy borders such as picture frames and coloured line borders. 'Shadow' allows you to add a drop shadow effect as if the text box is casting a shadow onto the slide.

To change the background colour of the textbox, click fill circled below left and select a colour from the drop down menu.

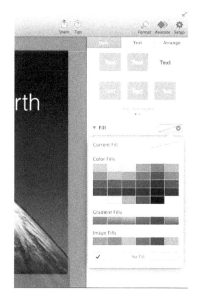 

Also if you want to add a border, under the border section click where it says 'no border' as shown above and change it to picture frame

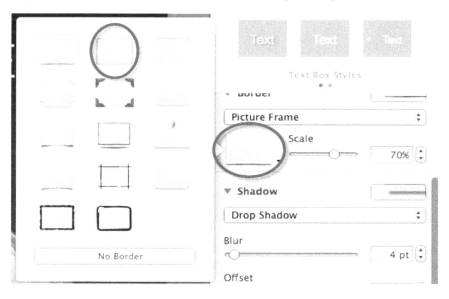

Click the 'choose frame style' button circled above and select a picture frame style from the menu that appears. Change the size by moving the scale slider.

Here is the result of the effect.

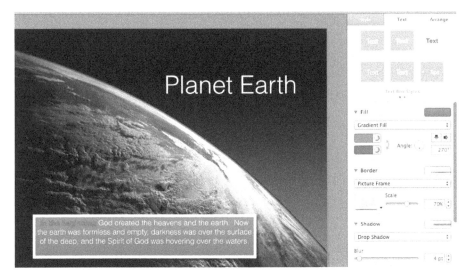

Saving

You can save your work onto your documents on your local mac or onto your iCloud Drive as with Pages.

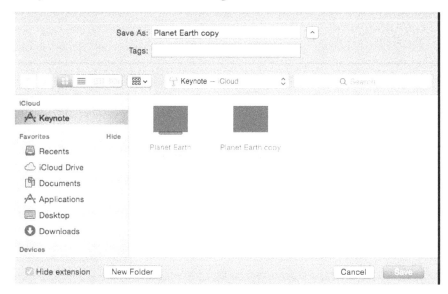

Down the left hand side of the screen you will see some destinations where you can save your file. Take note of Documents under favourites - this is on your mac. Also take note of iCloud at the top, this saves onto your iCloud Drive.

The advantage of saving to your iCloud Drive is you can access and edit the documents you have just been working on, on your iPhone or iPad. Or even another mac.

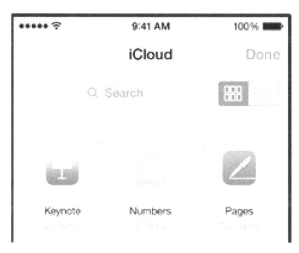

Chapter 8

Using Numbers

iWork (Apple Productivity Apps), is an office suite of applications that include

Pages; a desktop publishing and word-processing package,

Keynote for presentations

Numbers; a spreadsheet program.

If you don't have these applications on your Mac, you can download them from the App Store.

Lets take a look at creating a simple spreadsheet using numbers.

Starting Numbers

Numbers allows you to create spreadsheets. To numbers keynote, go to launch pad and click the numbers icon.

Once numbers has loaded, you can select a saved file to open.

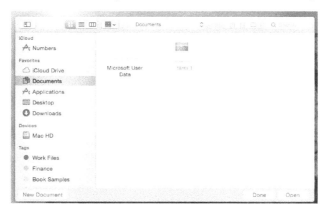

If you want to create a new spreadsheet, click 'new document' on the bottom left hand side of the window.

From here you can select from a variety of pre-designed templates with different themes, fonts and colours.

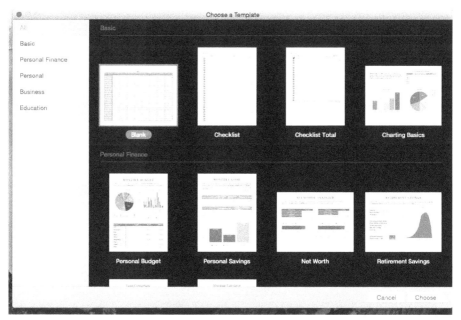

For this example use a blank sheet

Once you have selected a template you will see the main screen as shown below. This is where you can start building your spreadsheet.

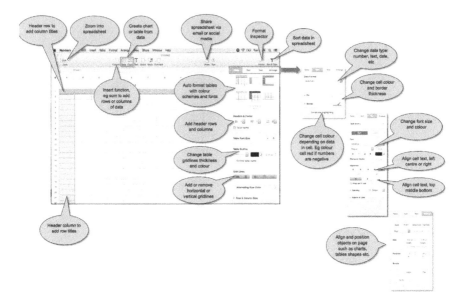

Building a Spreadsheet

To begin building your spreadsheet, enter the data into the cells. In this example we are going to build a basic invoice of costs of items

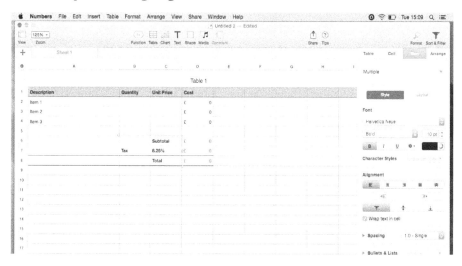

Entering Data

Enter the header cells into the grey row at the top of your spreadsheet. Then enter the rest of the data as shown above.

Change the total cells at the bottom to bold text.

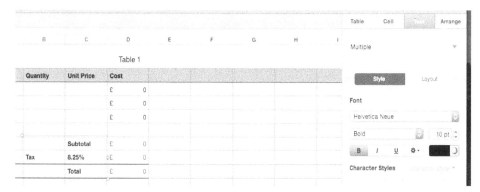

Do this by highlighting them with your mouse and from the cell tab on the right hand side of your screen click Bold.

Changing Data Types

Next highlight all the cells that will contain the prices for items, and make them a currency data type. Change it to Pound Sterling or US Dollar.

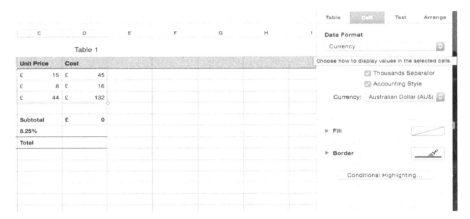

Do this by highlighting your cells as shown above, then from the cell tab on the right hand side, click in the dropdown box under 'data format' and select currency. Further down the tab you can change it to a specific currency depending on which country you are in.

Adding Formulas

Enter a formula to calculate the cost of each item. In the first cell under the heading 'cost' hit your equals sign to begin your formula. Click the cell under quantity, press the asterisk (*) then click the cell under unit price. This means you want to multiply the values in these two cells together.

Description	Quantity	Unit Price	Cost	
Item 1			= B2 ▾ × C2 ▾	✗ ✓
Item 2			£ 0	
Item 3			£ 0	
		Subtotal	£ 0	
	Tax	8.25%	£ 0	
		Total	£ 0	

Cost = Quantity * Unit Price.

Adding Functions

Now add a function to work out the total cost. For this one use the sum function to add all the values together.

Click in the cell next to subtotal and click the function icon on the tool bar at the top of the screen.

Select 'sum' from the drop down menu. The function will automatically highlight the values to add up.

If it doesn't click where it says D2:D5 this is the cells it will add up. Now select new the cells you want to add.

Saving

You can save your work onto your documents on your local mac or onto your iCloud Drive as with Pages.

Down the left hand side of the screen you will see some destinations where you can save your file. Take note of Documents under favourites - this is on your mac. Also take note of iCloud at the top, this saves onto your iCloud Drive.

The advantage of saving to your iCloud Drive is you can access and edit the documents you have just been working on, on your iPhone or iPad. Or even another mac.

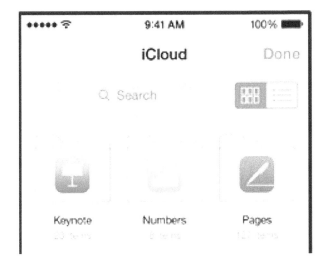

Security Considerations

Macs are said to have better security, however they are still susceptible to malware, phishing and viruses, so its wise to take precautions when browsing the web or opening emails.

Its a myth that Macs don't get viruses, so make sure you're protected, especially when you are shopping or banking online.

In this section we'll take a look at some of the security aspects of Macs and how to go about putting it into practice.

User Accounts

Open up the System Preferences on the apple menu.

I have found over the years that it is best to set up two separate accounts for yourself on your mac - one as a standard user and one as an administrator. You use the standard user for everyday use such as web browsing, email, photos, music and word processing etc. You use the administrator user to install new software or updates only never for normal use. The theory is that a standard user is not able to change system settings or malicious software is less likely to do any damage because of this. Administrators have full access to all settings and all files on the system making it a risky user account to use for normal use.

Click Users & Groups shown below.

This is how I have my macbook set up.

User: for normal use + my iCloud account

Admin: administrator for installing software and making system changes.

Guest User: Disable this.

Add a new user by first clicking the padlock and entering your password.

Then click the plus sign and enter your new user details

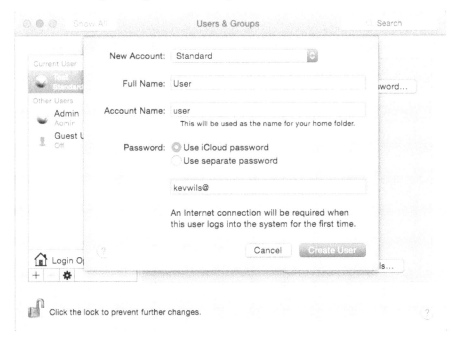

Hit create user. This is your standard user. Use it for normal use. Log out as your administrator account. You don't need to use this one anymore, if any settings need changing or you need to install anything, Mac OS will prompt you for the administrator password when you are logged in as your standard user.

Firewall

To set up your firewall, open the preferences App and go to go to 'Security & Privacy', click on the Firewall tab

Unlock the preference pane by clicking on the padlock,

Click the 'Turn On Firewall'.

Gatekeeper

Gatekeeper is a feature introduced in Mountain Lion and OS X Lion that checks for malware to help protect your Mac from misbehaving apps downloaded from the Internet.

You will find the settings in your System Preferences and Security & Privacy.

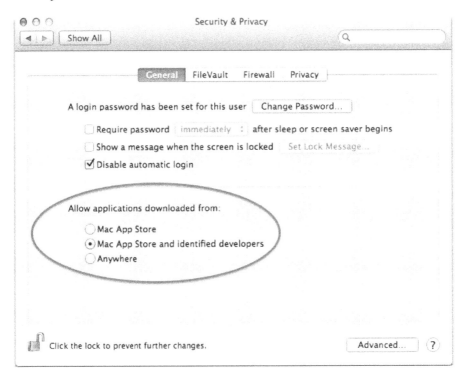

Do Apple Macs get Viruses?

Macs can get a virus, so the short answer to the question is Yes. However, the likelihood of an Mac user getting a virus when compared to a Microsoft Windows user is very little.

Although the Mac OS is more secure than many versions of Windows, any software, plug-ins, or other add-ons that are installed onto the computer that connect to the Internet can introduce their own security vulnerabilities. The most common ways to attack a Mac computer is through a third-party browser and browser plug-ins like Adobe Reader, Flash, and Java. Today, most Mac users have these plug-ins installed and enabled on the computer, but in doing so compromise the overall security of the system.

As Macs become more popular, more and more malware is being developed to target Mac OS, so even though Macs are secure, make sure you are protected.

Finally, although a Mac computer is less susceptible to viruses, you can still be a victim of Trojan horses, phishing, and other online fraud.

There is no such thing as a 100% safe computer, a Mac, Windows, and even Linux are all capable of being infected with a virus or other malware.

A free simple anti virus for mac is Avast. There are a lot of different ones out there, but this one is free, small, fast and up to date. It is a good place to start. It has a web shield to help you when you are browsing the web and warns you about websites. It also has a email shield that scans incoming emails for threats.

You can download it here.

```
http://www.avast.com/en-gb/index-mac
```

Once on their website, click the download link.

Click download now.

Go to the downloads folder in your finder.

Double click `avast_free_antivirus_mac_setup.dmg`

Follow the instructions on screen.